Cosmological

Transformation

Enlightening Thoughts Vol. 6

By Ron Bracale

Cosmological Transformation

ISBN: 978-1-941090-02-2

Published by

Enlightening Treasures

Conneaut, OH

Enlightening Thoughts

Vol. 1: Knowledge of Love

Vol. 2: Healing Love

Vol. 3: Spiritual Love

Vol. 4: True Love

Vol. 5: Being Love

Vol. 6: Cosmological Transformation

This is a collection of modern haiku...

Turn off your thinking analytical mind...

Seek to feel with your inner being...

Become present with the words...

Enlightenment is a verb, not an attainment...

Enlightenment is a state of Being Love...

We are all travelling together...

We are all in relationship within the whole...

Cosmological Transformation

the bamboo whispers

seas of humanity roar

nature's ways endure

~ ~ ~

quiet spoken truth

boisterous market hawkers

noise drowns out signals

~ ~ ~

glittering glamor

entrancing ego's visions

time breaks the dark spell

wind in the bamboo

gentle as ro dai meri

formless teaches form

~   ~   ~

the day is so long

and in the end it's too short

fulfill your essence

~   ~   ~

spending day and night

longing for so many things

flow nature's cycles

dear burning flower

external quickly changes

beauty in a flash

~ ~ ~

time the true teacher

Internal Essence untouched

trickster fate unveils

~ ~ ~

Ah: Deep in Belly

Om: Earth-Sky Light Surrounding

All One Infinite

Listen to the Sound

Words diminish Reality

Within, the Essence

~ ~ ~

the Earthly Journey

Awakening within Form

Visiting for Love

~ ~ ~

Shining beyond Time

Separation's Illusion

Body-Mind clothes Me

each Soul is Unique

dimly reflected in Life

each Soul is precious

~ ~ ~

immortal danger

humanity's paradox

all things pass away

~ ~ ~

fear and stress abound

deny we are visiting

dreams before our light

wrestling with what self

ego defending its lies

be humbly human

~ ~ ~

guardians watching

telepathic revealers

hiding is over

~ ~ ~

Nowhere to go to

be fluid, go with the flow,

only Here to Grow…

Mental Projection

Filtering Sensory Stream

Interpreting All

~ ~ ~

Longing for Union

Transcendent Reality

Essence beyond Form

~ ~ ~

Time and Energy

Authentic Priority

Empower Yourself

Manifest your Dream

Incarnation's True purpose

Crystal Clear Intent

~ ~ ~

Sensory Streams Flow

the Watcher never Changes

Dancing Together

~ ~ ~

Illusion of Self

Being is Relationship

Intertwined as One

Trickery of Words

Reality of Feelings

Experience Now

~ ~ ~

Stalking Wisdom's Pearl

Capturing the Real Essence

Becoming Freedom

~ ~ ~

Releasing Control

Learning with Experience

Accepting what Is

we are Messengers

every Feeling, Dream, Thought, Word

is our Reflection

~ ~ ~

Message in Motion

Gather, Process, and Transmit

in our Expression

~ ~ ~

Life tells a Story

all we do tells a Story

is Life your Story?

Hungry for Input

Stimulation to Process

Sensory Data

~ ~ ~

Trinary Nature:

Mystery, Duality,

within Unity.

~ ~ ~

the Totality

Unknown and Unknowable

Experience Now

Fire of Desire

disturbing Tranquility

Teasing us Forward

~ ~ ~

Moving in Time's Game

the Illusion of Control

the Trickster Fate Laughs

~ ~ ~

wanting and needing

Constrained by Natural Law

Death keeping the Way

all Living Beings

Rising and Falling like Waves

Touching Mystery

~ ~ ~

Happiness Sadness

Waves on the shoreline passing

move forward with Love

~ ~ ~

Beauty Manifest

showing Nature's Sweet Glory

Flowers in Season

Old passes for New

that Greater may manifest

Endless Potential

~ ~ ~

no Focus on Self

look around and show your Love

move Free in the Flow

~ ~ ~

Ambition and Dreams

Relationships beyond Self

Expand our Being

Expectations fail

disappointment's precursor

have None and Be Free

~ ~ ~

Boldly Authentic

maintaining Integrity

Expressing your Self

~ ~ ~

satisfied or not:

it's in your mind: not body

Judging Conditions

Mind is Fantasy

Body is Real Energy

Door to Mystery

~ ~ ~

Mental Structure's Cloth

Tree of Belief's Filtering

Us from Sensations

~ ~ ~

Telepathic Web

discordant spectrum of Minds

billions of voices

Humanities' Dream

Melody in Harmony

Singing Together

~ ~ ~

waiting for future

missing Today slipping by

then your Time is Done

~ ~ ~

Ponder Infinity

Forever beyond Reason

to Fill with Wonder

Life is in Motion

Nature Forever Changing

Dancing with the Flow

~ ~ ~

Entrancing Dramas

Circles Trapping Attention

Escape from the Web

~ ~ ~

Freedom from Bondage

Invisible Walls Confuse

Hidden Doors waiting

Maze of Life Pathways

sorting through Endless Options

seeking Freedom's Way

~ ~ ~

darkness covers Earth

surrender to Being True

nothing more to do

~ ~ ~

Grateful for the day

Honoring Life's Precious Gift

Thankful for the night

Galaxy is vast

eons of Time have Played Out

Surprises Await

~ ~ ~

Edge of Time reveals

Continually the New

Stories that Unfold

~ ~ ~

Humanities Dream

Historical Memes Breeding

needing to be Purged

Unconscious Pathways

Shock upon Awakening

Galaxy Beckons

~ ~ ~

Patterns of Nature

Golden Mean Fractal Designs

Optimized for Life

~ ~ ~

Evolving Life Forms

Enthalpy Complexity

Growing Consciousness

Systems Interact

most Elegant Solutions

Profoundly Simple

~   ~   ~

Extinction Pruning

Tree of Life Branches Onward

Surviving Test of Time

~   ~   ~

Synchronicity

the Universe shows the Way

Lessons of Power

Magic Sound of Flute

Dancing of Notes and Silence

Resonating Space

~ ~ ~

Melody Transcends

Notes Rolling on the Shoreline

Edge of the Present

~ ~ ~

Music is the Key

Unlocking the Mysteries

Letting the Heart Hear

Revealing Emotion

Communicating Feeling

Talking Soul to Soul

~ ~ ~

Boundaries Dissolve

Sound Envelops Listeners

Communing as One

~ ~ ~

Tranquility Now

Where only the Soul Exists

Serenity Now

Sacred Melodies

Mirror Divine Energies

Connecting to Source

~ ~ ~

Original Note

Fills the Void with Everything

Calling us back Home

~ ~ ~

when Myths come Alive

Ancient Gods visit again

Ancestors Awake

Memories buried

Embedded Symbols sleep

Humanities' Heart

~ ~ ~

Cities under Seas

Collective Amnesia

Figments breaking through

~ ~ ~

useless denial

Old Stories based on the Truth

coming into Light

Rediscovery

redefining History

Revealing our past

~ ~ ~

present foolishness

forced into contemplation

Wisdom Awakens

~ ~ ~

Viral Parasite

Memes in Mental Programming

mislead us from Love

Human Global Dream

Contaminated with Self

Surrender to Love

~ ~ ~

The I is a Lie

there's only Us Together

Living Relations

~ ~ ~

Melt into the Earth

Astral Traveler Freedom

Soar among the Stars

Purification

Winds of our fates Winnowing

Clarity Remains

~ ~ ~

Spirit of Service

Touching Someone's Deep Feelings

sharing Compassion

~ ~ ~

Quiet in our Mind

Imagination Drifting

Witnessing Dream-Time

Chromatic World View

Elements not Opposites

Complimentary

~ ~ ~

Mind Theorizes

Winds of Fate weave Spirit Dreams

Infinity Laughs

~ ~ ~

All is Mystery

Endless Wonder to Behold

Natural Designs

Incarnation's Web

Perceivers seeking Freedom

Weaving through the Dream

~ ~ ~

don't let it scare you

you have No Control at all

be True to your Self

~ ~ ~

Everything we Know

all of our Belief Systems

Filter Reality

Living in your Mind

Overshadows Mystery

Present Perception

~ ~ ~

Truth is Fantastic

Sensory Experience

Mind Cannot Fathom

~ ~ ~

Fiction looks like Fact

Mental Illusions Confuse

Essence Dancing on

Eyes Deep as the Sea

like my Ancient Memory

Cries to Let it Be

~ ~ ~

Soothing in the flow

no Resistance to Spirit

Refresh in the know

~ ~ ~

Void does not Exist

Everywhere Vibrations Drone

Ethereal Spirit

Within Infinity

Consciousness in each Center

Dreaming Creation

~   ~   ~

Fabric of Life Threads

Present in Eternity

Together Dancing

~   ~   ~

Fate and Destiny

Alone and yet Together

Dancing Life with Love

Each Second is New

You are the Crest of a Wave

Free to be Yourself

~ ~ ~

addicted to stuff

Consciousness gets tangled there

compromised Being

~ ~ ~

Universe Echoes

Returning our Reflection

Shine your Brilliant Love

Keeping the Rhythm

Being in a Timeless State

the Flow Dancing Us

~ ~ ~

Artfully live Love

Relish your Human Nature

Be your Humble Self

~ ~ ~

Harmoniously

Balanced Relationships

Not divided: One

Embrace the Journey

Being Whole, Fully Human

Marvelous Living

~ ~ ~

False Intelligence

Nature is Divine Wisdom

Flow the Cosmic Way

~ ~ ~

luscious springtime air

reinvigorating body

heavenly passions

the Truth of my youth

metamorphosis refines

Truth never static

~ ~ ~

Dark Mystery Life

myriad forms flow the Way

birth – form – changes - death

~ ~ ~

crystalline splendor

only humans see the Gift

Gateway to Wonder

Spirit whispers Love

Silently eyes tell it all

Deeper than our form

~ ~ ~

ringing in silence

a presence deeper than words

unspoken feelings

~ ~ ~

Fractalizing Void

Sentient Living Basis

everything's prime Source

Words recount the past

Experiences here now

Embrace each Instant

~ ~ ~

Words paint a picture

pictures filter sensations

Present is richness

~ ~ ~

ideas are ghosts

preconceptions mislead Now

Being flowing Now

mental illusion

Everyone in their own world

while Reality Waits

~ ~ ~

E.T. Watching us

Humanity in Disgrace

Time to Change our Song

~ ~ ~

stress and worrying

pre-civilized Age of fear

Return a New Dream

Entangled Spirits

we need Love from each other

Nurturing Comfort

~ ~ ~

Demand Peace on Earth

no power to terrorize

Self-Empowerment

~ ~ ~

Protect Innocents

that the Gentle may Flourish

Manifest Beauty

Wake up in the Dream

Dimensional Expansion

Reveals the Hidden

~ ~ ~

Transcend all Boundaries

Open Superstring Portals

Mysteries Await

~ ~ ~

Endless Mystery

Experience pure and free

Emotional bliss

the Meaning of Life

Words twist in Endless Circles

Embrace Mystery

~ ~ ~

Guiding our Life Path

Analyze Information

Journey in Wonder

~ ~ ~

Illusions Surround

Deeply Rooted Assumptions

Not Being Present

Mentally Knowing

Ideas Hide Reality

Remember Feeling

~ ~ ~

Without an Answer

Myriad Questions Screaming

Feel Changes Coming

~ ~ ~

Mother Earth Moaning

Words and Ideas Falter

How are We Living?

Cosmic Interplay

Psychic Battleground Within

Follow Love's Guidance

~ ~ ~

Complicated Choice

Countless Factors Interleave

Nature's Way Calling

~ ~ ~

Personal Journey

What can be Expressed and Shared

Words are not Feelings

Intense Inner Space

Mind Races, Death stalks and laughs

our Feelings Matter

~ ~ ~

Essence of Being

not Memories of the Past

Shining in the Now

~ ~ ~

Consciousness Touches

Radiating our Feelings

Inside Each Other

Entangled as One

Dancing Relationships Flow

Gliding with the Winds

~ ~ ~

what is important

the People you Relate to

Shared Memories

~ ~ ~

Meta-Entangled

Silver Cords wound together

Consciousness Entwined

AH and OM cycle

Sacred Space in Living Breath

embrace Inner Peace

~ ~ ~

Symbols in the Sky

revealing Signs and Omens

Prophesy Warnings

~ ~ ~

Mythical moments

Woven into the Dream-Time

World View shattering

always distracted

Center Light transcends Boundaries

encompassing All

~ ~ ~

self-luminous Void

Creative Fractal Present

New under the Sun

~ ~ ~

not Inferior

all People Unique with Gifts

not Superior

Vain and Arrogant

I don't follow those rules

Be Enlightenment

~ ~ ~

unsettling koan

lose your assumptions to Grow

Luminous Bird Flies

~ ~ ~

Waves of Breath Cycle

Lapping on the Present Shore

Patterns in the Sands

Breather and the Breath

Boundaries Illusions Fading

Spring Breezes Refresh

~ ~ ~

Being is Present

Perceptions are of the Past

Sunshine Memories

~ ~ ~

Authentic Being

Unique, Intending Choices

Relationships Dance

Resonate History

of Ancestor's Momentum

Drumming a New Beat

~ ~ ~

the fashion of Art

Stylistic Aesthetics

Fractal a New Branch

~ ~ ~

Meta-Entangled

Biosphere Strings, complex Web

Sights along the Trail

Dreams for our Future

Intend Collective Vision

Birds singing in Trees

~ ~ ~

Shakuhachi sings

Journey of Enlightenment

Traditions Evolve

~ ~ ~

Being Luminous

Consciousness Shining in Strings

Eyes touching the Stars

Perceiving the Past

while Being in the Present

Intend Bright Futures

~ ~ ~

Countless Choices are

Encompassing Constraints Call

Nature's Way Teaches

~ ~ ~

Endless Intentions

Cooperative Power

Play in Harmony

Expose Emotions

Heal Interactions with Love

Smiles are strong Magic

~ ~ ~

Envy not others' Lives

it would not fit Unique You

let your Nature Speak

~ ~ ~

Strumming Superstrings

Brightening Group Consciousness

Dust in a Sunbeam

Auras overlap

Intensify with Coherence

Dreaming Together

~ ~ ~

Prophesy of Doom

Time has its own Ideas

laugh at the folly

~ ~ ~

Seek to be Cosmic

Everyone Dreams Together

a play of billions

everyone mortal

Forever Present in Change

space around a vase

~ ~ ~

Traveler's Mission

in Strange Lands without a Map

share with all you meet

~ ~ ~

Feel your Way around

enticed by the Mystical

a Loving touch Heals

ideas collide

minds will never be as One

Hearts melt Together

~   ~   ~

Celestial Rhythm

Spiraling from birth to death

don't lean on a Wheel

~   ~   ~

Life's precious Treasure

Earth's Living Diversity

birds sing together

Passions in our minds

what do we give Power to

Hearts expressing Love

~ ~ ~

no hiding Within

telepathic revealing

naked open book

~ ~ ~

Now how do you Feel

what are you Radiating

Dreams are a Mirror

Gentle with Yourself

nurture Brilliant Splendor

fumbling and laughing

~ ~ ~

Special and Unique

but not more so than others

Flowers in a Field

~ ~ ~

Genuine Nature

Whole within the Vast Cosmos

Hummingbird's travels

Finding in One's Self

Shining Natural Glory

still water Reflects

~ ~ ~

Cycling of Fortunes

Touching, not trying to grasp

river flowing by

~ ~ ~

behind appearance

the Deep Mystery abides

Stories in Symbols

names fragment Vision

Nature is not Mosaic

all strands form One Web

~ ~ ~

deep Realization

endless layers of Meaning

greatest Gift is Love

~ ~ ~

Genuine Nature

May you be Fully Human

you only need Love

www.ingramcontent.com/pod-product-compliance
Lightning Source LLC
Chambersburg PA
CBHW071848020426
42331CB00007B/1917